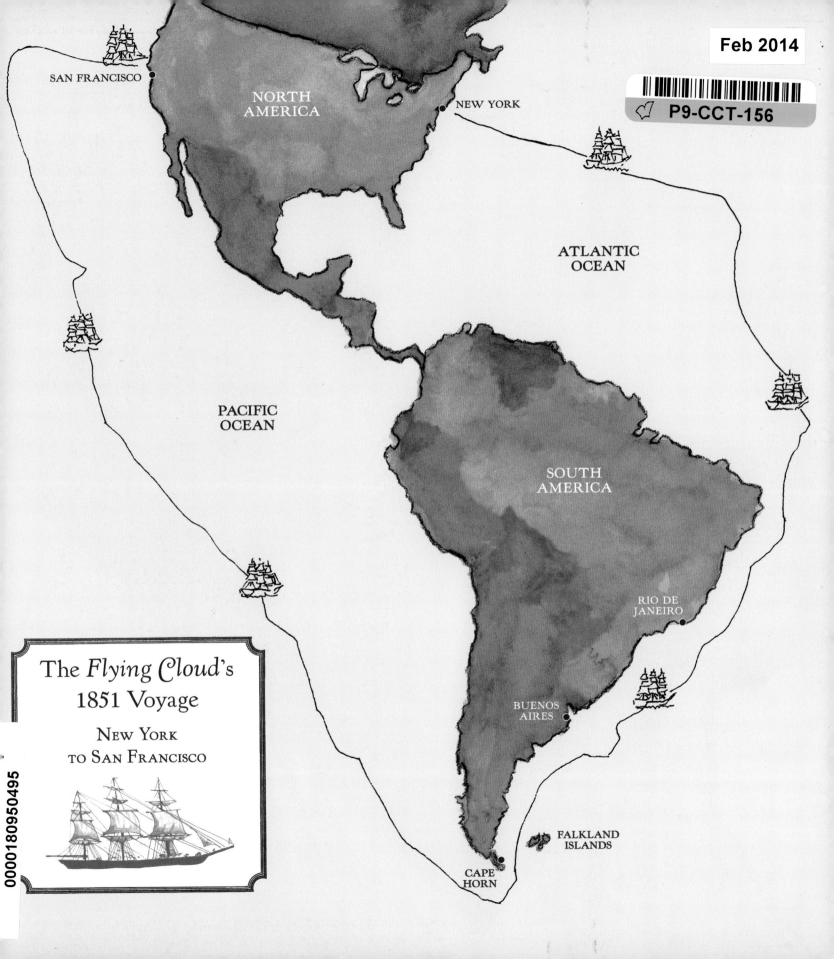

SAN FRANCISCO

NORTH
AMERICA

NEW YORK

ATLANTIC
OCEAN

PACIFIC
OCEAN

SOUTH
AMERICA

RIO DE
JANEIRO

BUENOS
AIRES

FALKLAND
ISLANDS

CAPE
HORN

The *Flying Cloud's*
1851 Voyage

NEW YORK
TO SAN FRANCISCO

Dare the Wind

Tracey Fern

Pictures by

Emily
Arnold
McCully

MARGARET FERGUSON BOOKS

Farrar Straus Giroux
New York

Ellen Prentiss had always felt the sea tug at her heart, strong as a full-moon tide. Her papa said that was because she was born with saltwater in her veins.

While other girls spent their days stitching samplers and sweeping floors, Ellen spent her days at the shore in Marblehead, Massachusetts. She chased the waves. She raced the wind. She watched great sailing ships skim over wide endless water. And she dreamed of living her life at sea and catching her share of adventure.

As soon as her papa's trading schooner glided into port, Ellen rushed aboard for sailing lessons. Most people thought her papa was a fool, teaching a girl the ways of the sea. But Papa was born with saltwater in his veins, too.

He taught Ellen how to hoist a sail and splice a rope. He taught her how to tack against the wind and turn the wheel. Then he taught her something that most sailors and even some captains never learned. He taught her how to navigate.

"Hoist it to your shoulder, Ellen, and look for the sun," Papa said as he put his sextant in her hands. "Now, move the sextant's arm until the sun sits in the middle of the mirror like a picture in a frame."

"I've got it!" Ellen cried. She scribbled the measurements from the sextant and the time from the chronometer on a chip of slate. Ellen worked for hours by the kitchen fire, learning the complicated calculations needed to navigate a ship.

Then, every chance she could, she navigated Papa's schooner beyond the rocky arms of Marblehead Harbor. She practiced until she could find her way far out at sea with no landmarks to guide her. She practiced until she had the sunburned cheeks and wide step of a seasoned sailor. By the time she was a young lady, Ellen had practiced so much she could race the fishing fleet across Massachusetts Bay—and beat it!

"Catch me if you dare!" Ellen shouted to every ship she passed, as she shot through changing tides and slipped over rocky shallows.

"Slow down, Ellen, and watch the wind and water," Papa always said when she returned to shore. "A true navigator must have the caution to read the sea, as well as the courage to dare the wind."

As soon as Ellen met a man who loved the sea as much as she did, she married him.

For ten years, Ellen and Perkins Creesy sailed sturdy ships on safe routes, Ellen as navigator and Perkins as captain. Then Perkins got command of a new clipper, the *Flying Cloud*.

Surely she's the most glorious ship afloat, Ellen thought
when she first walked up the gangplank of the *Flying Cloud*
as it lay docked in New York Harbor.

The clipper's soaring masts, her sleek decks, her bow as sharp as a sailmaker's needle—they were all made to improve the clipper's speed! Ellen knew they would need every bit of that speed on their maiden voyage—a fifteen-thousand-mile journey from New York City down to Cape Horn at the tip of South America and up to San Francisco—racing to get passengers and cargo to the Gold Rush.

If Ellen and Perkins could make the trip faster than any ship ever had, they would receive a bonus—and bragging rights as the best sailors in the world. It was the adventure Ellen had always dreamed of catching!

Finally, the day of departure arrived: June 2, 1851. The crew sang as they hoisted sails:

A Yankee ship comes down the river,
Blow, bully boys, blow!
Her mast and spars, they shine like silver,
Blow, my bully boys, blow!

The anchor rose with a clang. The shimmering white sails snapped taut. The *Flying Cloud* was away!

Ellen stood on deck and let the rhythm of the rolling boards settle in her bones. She wrapped her shawl close, raised the cold brass spyglass to her eye, and turned to face the unknown.

The murky coastal water changed to bottomless blue as the *Flying Cloud* sailed into the open sea, where the water met the sky. Now Ellen had nothing but the sun, the moon, and the stars to guide her.

Each day at dawn, at noon, and at twilight, Ellen lifted her sextant from its flannel nest and took her measurements. In the evening, she went belowdecks to the great oak table, where she ran her daily calculations. She marked the ship's position on her chart. She noted the distance they had traveled, counting from noon one day to noon the next as a full day at sea. "We covered 164 miles our first day out, 145 miles on our second day, and 228 miles on our third," Ellen told Perkins as she marked her chart. Then she studied her wind and current guides. Finally, she plotted a course to catch the strongest wind and current she could.

A *fast course*, Ellen thought, *fast enough to beat every ship on the water!*

Ellen pushed the ship even faster.

"We went 293 miles!" Ellen told Perkins the next day.

The masts creaked and groaned their song as the *Flying Cloud*
rushed on: *Hurry, hurry, hurry!* Soon every twist of rope and thread
of canvas was stretched taut.

"Catch me if you dare!" Ellen shouted to the wind as she leaned far
out over the bow, the sea sparkling green and white around her and
ten thousand yards of canvas stretched high and wide above her.

Then on the fifth day, Ellen heard a tremendous noise. Suddenly, the ship shuddered and tipped sideways. Another crash rang out, then the shouts and pounding boots of the crew.

Ellen raced to mid-ship.

No! Not my glorious ship! Ellen thought, her face turning white as whalebone when she saw the ruin.

The mainmast had broken. The sails hung in ribbons. The deck was littered with splinters of pine, shreds of canvas, and bits of iron.

Perkins and the crew worked all through the day and night fixing the mast, patching the sails, and sweeping the deck. During that time, Ellen could only worry and wonder: Had her daring pushed the ship too hard?

For the next few weeks, Ellen set a cautious course, catching gentler breezes. The *Flying Cloud* traveled only 137 miles one day, 171 miles the next.

Then the wind slackened further. The waves slowed. The sails hung limp. The crew grew quiet and the passengers grew restless. The *Flying Cloud* drifted for days on the glassy sea.

Calm, calm, calm, Perkins scrawled angrily in his logbook.

Ellen had steered the ship into the doldrums, the mysterious areas of calm around the equator that had plagued sailors for thousands of years.

Belowdecks at her chart table, Ellen studied a new book on navigation. It promised a path through the doldrums close to the coast of Brazil. That was a dangerous route. Ellen knew there were shoals along that coast that could turn good ships into ghost ships. But if she did nothing, the ship might drift hundreds of miles off course.

Then Ellen remembered what her papa had taught her long ago: a true navigator must have the caution to read the sea, as well as the courage to dare the wind.

There is no glory in second place, Ellen thought. *Now is the time for courage.*

Ellen set a course to hug the coast and let the currents pull the ship toward shore. Finally she spotted a ripple of dark water ahead. Wind!

Slowly the sails filled. Soon the breeze was blowing a steady stream that tousled Ellen's hair and ruffled her dress. Ellen's new route led the ship out of the doldrums.

The *Flying Cloud* flew on down the coast of South America, past Rio de Janeiro, Buenos Aires, and the Falkland Islands. By day fifty, Cape Horn loomed ahead.

Cape Horn—the words turned the sailors' faces grim.

"The Devil's best mess," they worried. "Nothing but swift tides, uncharted shoals, and the jagged jaws of shipwrecks."

Clouds piled up like black cotton, and thunder boomed like cannon fire. Wind howled through the masts, and waves crashed onto the deck. Soon the ship was lost in the endless gray of sea and sky and snow. Ellen couldn't see the sun, so she couldn't use her sextant.

Now is the time for caution, she thought. *I can still read the sea.*

Ellen lashed herself to the rail and peered at the ship's wake through flashes of lightning. Usually the thin band of white water shot straight out behind the ship. Now the wake angled sharply out to sea. Ellen knew this meant that the wind and waves were pushing the ship sideways through the sea toward the rocky coast! Turning back would cost them some dear time, but Ellen didn't hesitate.

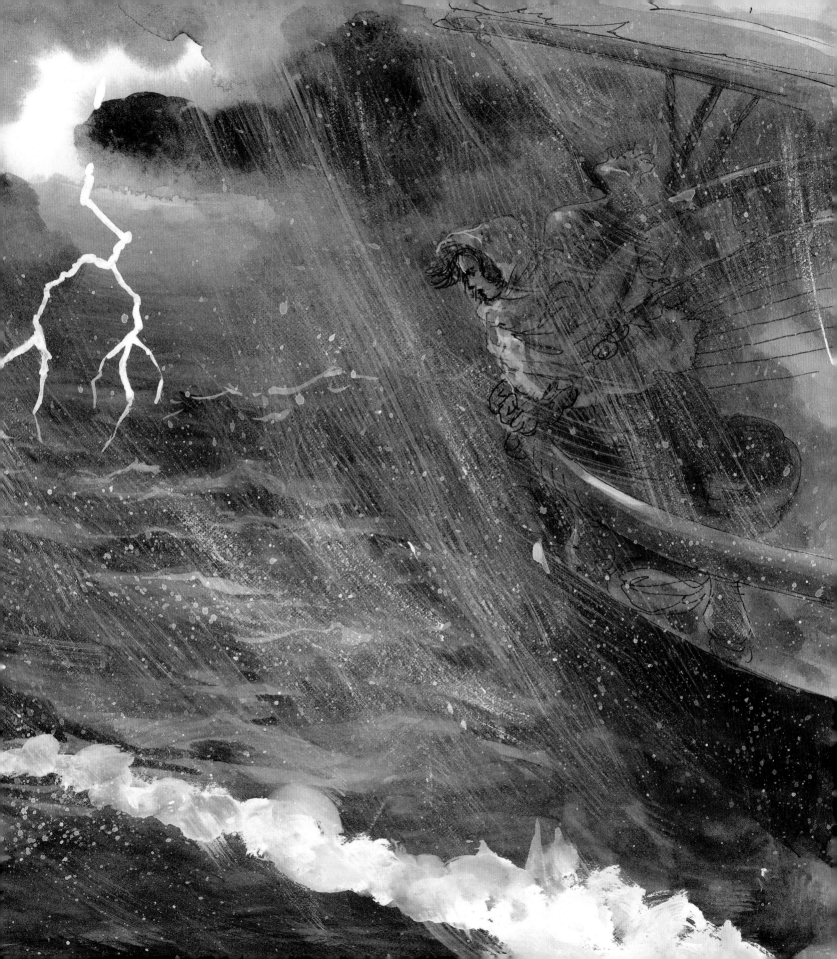

She untied her ropes. Then, hand over hand, Ellen crept along the rail to Perkins.

"I've read the wake, Perkins!" Ellen cried. "Turn north or we'll be dashed to bits!"

"Hard about!" Perkins bellowed.

Two helmsmen hung on the wheel, slowly turning the clipper through the eye of the wind.

Ellen stood at the rail until the sleet froze her dress stiff and the ice glazed her hair like crystal. For two days, she fought the gale. Finally the wind eased. The rain slowed. The waves flattened. The ship was safe.

Ellen guided the ship south again. The *Flying Cloud* slipped around the ice-covered cliffs of Cape Horn and surged north through the Pacific.

Day after day, Ellen rode the wind, keeping a careful watch on the mended mast. Faster, faster, faster—300, 350, 400 miles a day. Would the mast hold? Ellen sped past schooners and sloops and brigs and barks. Finally on the morning of August 31, 1851, she heard the cry she had been waiting for: "Land ho! Land ho!"

Ellen's heart raced like a riptide as she watched the red hills of San Francisco rise slowly over the horizon. She had done it! She had brought her ship and crew to port safely—and faster than she had ever dreamed.

"Eighty-nine days, Ellen—a world record!" Perkins said, laughing as he lifted her high. "I've never known a sailor or a seabird who could find the wind like you!"

On the piers and in the warehouses, sailors whispered that Ellen must have put magic in the masts. But Ellen was a true navigator, just as her papa had taught her to be. She knew her magic was the caution to read the sea and the courage to dare the wind.

AUTHOR'S NOTE

Dare the Wind is based on a true story. Eleanor "Ellen" Prentiss was born in Marblehead, Massachusetts, in 1814. Her father, John Prentiss, was the captain of a coastal trading schooner and most likely taught her navigation because he did not have any sons to follow in his footsteps. After Ellen married Josiah Perkins Creesy in 1841, she spent years honing her skills navigating Perkins's merchant ships on the trade route to China. Then thousands of Americans began heading west to California in the Gold Rush of 1849. The journey across the continent to California by wagon could take six to eight months. The trip around Cape Horn in an older ship could take four to eight months. Clipper ships cut that time in half. And the faster a ship reached California, the sooner it delivered its passengers, sold its cargo, made a profit, earned some glory, and returned to sell more goods. Ellen and Perkins joined the race to earn some of that profit and glory with the *Flying Cloud*.

The *Flying Cloud*, built by naval architect Donald McKay of East Boston, Massachusetts, was an "extreme" clipper. It had a long, narrow hull, a sharp, pointed bow, and towering masts that were designed for speed. But Ellen wasn't content to rely only on the design of the clipper. She also studied wind and current data from a controversial new book by U.S. Navy Lieutenant Matthew Fontaine Maury.

Maury had compiled information from the logs of hundreds of ships and used it to plot shipping routes. In many cases, Maury's routes were very different from those traditionally used by navigators. Ellen decided to take the risk and follow Maury's new scientific approach to navigation.

Ellen's decision paid off. At a time when it was nearly unheard of for a woman to navigate a ship, Ellen's voyage of 89 days, 21 hours beat the record by more than 30 days and lasted for three years. Then Ellen broke her own record, steering the *Flying Cloud* from New York to San Francisco in 89 days, 8 hours. No wooden ship or iron windjammer ever bested her time.

Ellen rode the waves with Perkins until 1868, when he became ill. A few years later, Perkins died, steam replaced sail, and the last of the great clippers was gone. Ellen died on August 25, 1900, in Salem, Massachusetts.

If you would like to learn more about the Creesys and the first voyage of the *Flying Cloud*, see David W. Shaw's book, *Flying Cloud: The True Story of America's Most Famous Clipper Ship and the Woman Who Guided Her* (New York: William Morrow, 2000). For more information about the *Flying Cloud* and clippers in general, see The Maritime History Virtual Archive Web site at www.bruzelius.info /Nautica/Nautica.html and A.B.C. Whipple's *Clipper Ships* (Alexandria, Va.: Time-Life Books, 1980). Personal accounts of the journey and Perkins's log can be found in Margaret Lyon and Flora Elizabeth Reynolds's *The Flying Cloud and Her First Passengers* (Oakland, Calif.: Center for the Book, Mills College, 1992) as well as on the Web site The Era of the Clipper Ships at www.eraoftheclipperships.com.

GLOSSARY

BOW: The front of a ship.

CHRONOMETER: An extremely accurate clock used to help calculate a ship's position at sea.

LOGBOOK: A book used to record the ship's daily course, the wind direction, the weather, and other details.

MAINMAST: The tallest mast, usually in the middle of a three-masted ship such as the *Flying Cloud*.

MAST: A tall wooden pole or spar set upright on the deck and used to hold the rigging and sails.

SEXTANT: An instrument that measures the altitude or angle of the sun, the moon, or the stars above the horizon to help determine a ship's position at sea.

TACK: To change the direction of a sailing ship by turning the bow through the wind and shifting the sails to bring the wind from one side to the other.

WAKE: The waves, track, or path that a ship leaves behind when it moves through the water.

WHEEL: A mechanism used to help steer a ship.

For Doug, Samantha, and Ali
—T.F.

For BG and Raya
—E.A.M.

Farrar Straus Giroux Books for Young Readers
175 Fifth Avenue, New York 10010

Text copyright © 2014 by Tracey Fern
Pictures copyright © 2014 by Emily Arnold McCully
All rights reserved
Color separations by Bright Arts (H.K.) Ltd.
Printed in China by Toppan Leefung Printing,
Dongguan City, Guangdong Province
First edition, 2014
1   3   5   7   9   10   8   6   4   2

mackids.com

Library of Congress Cataloging-in-Publication Data
Fern, Tracey E.
    Dare the wind / Tracey Fern ; pictures by Emily Arnold McCully.
        pages cm
    ISBN 978-0-374-31699-0 (hardcover)
    1. Creesy, Eleanor, 1814–1900—Juvenile literature.   2. Flying Cloud (Clipper-ship)—Juvenile literature.
    3. Women sailors—Biography—Juvenile literature.   I. McCully, Emily Arnold, illustrator.   II. Title.

G478.C74F47 2014
387.5092—dc23
[B]
                                                                                        2013007868

With thanks to William N. Peterson, Curator Emeritus at Mystic Seaport, for his review and assistance.

Farrar Straus Giroux Books for Young Readers may be purchased for business or promotional use. For
information on bulk purchases please contact Macmillan Corporate and Premium Sales Department at
(800) 221-7945 x5442 or by email at specialmarkets@macmillan.com.

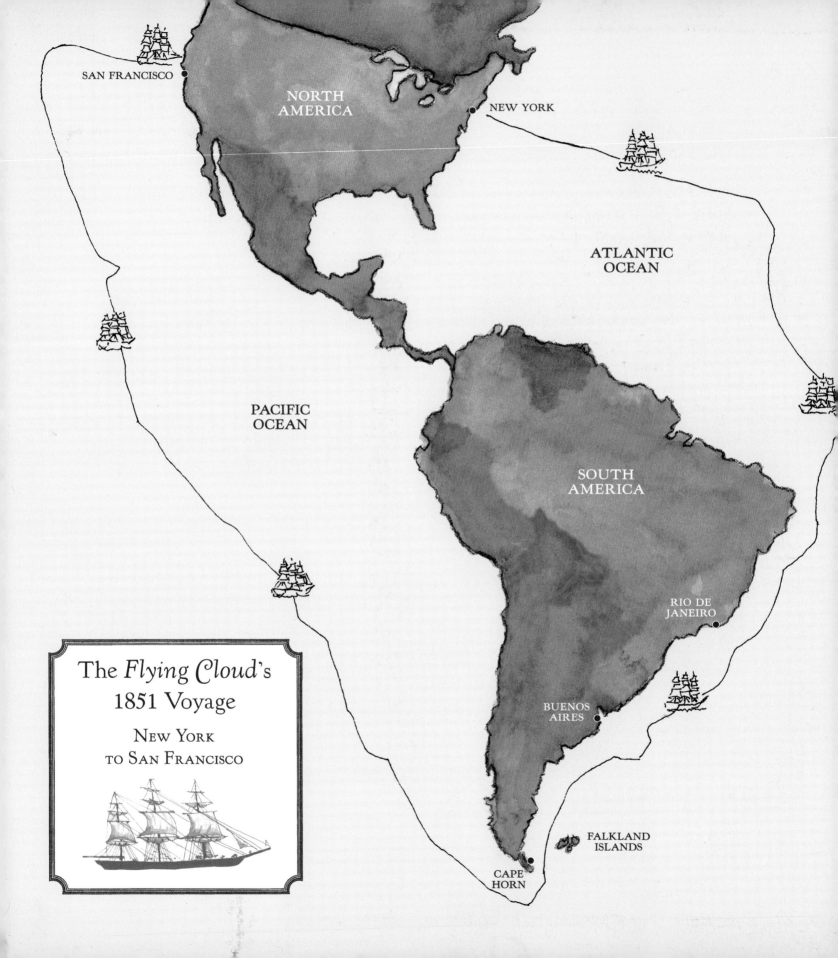

SAN FRANCISCO

NORTH
AMERICA

NEW YORK

ATLANTIC
OCEAN

PACIFIC
OCEAN

SOUTH
AMERICA

RIO DE
JANEIRO

BUENOS
AIRES

FALKLAND
ISLANDS

CAPE
HORN

The *Flying Cloud*'s
1851 Voyage

NEW YORK
TO SAN FRANCISCO